©2025 Joanne Sherry Mitchell. All rights reserved
Including the right to reproduce this book or
Portions thereof in any form whatsoever,
Without permission in writing from the publisher.
Printed in the United States of America.

Moments Swirling In Time

BY

JOANNE SHERRY MITCHELL

BOOKS BY JOANNE SHERRY MITCHELL

Moments
Moments And Then Some
Moments When Night Becomes Day
Moments Gentle Hints to Life
Moments Not Things
Moments No Replacement Found
Moments With Mrs. Melissa Sherry Smith 5th Grade Class
Moments Treasured
Momentos De Risa, Dolor y Amor
Moments As Milestones
Πολύτιμες Στιγμές
The Pain We Call Love
Moments Encountered
Moments Swirling In Time

Visit Joanne Mitchell's website

www.momentsbyjoanne.com

Email: moments@momentsbyjoanne.com

Acknowledgements

Cover Art by local artist, Davon Dirosier

Cover edits by Victor Morales, Art Director Professional Management, Inc.

With special thanks for their assistance in bringing this book to completion to:

        Betty Smith

        Marie Bartlett

Illustrations

A special thank you and recognition to
DAVON DIROSIER
a Miami, Florida Artist who illustrated beautifully my poems.

There Always	page xiii
We Kissed	page 10
A Solar Flare	page 14
I Came In	page 18
Cats Have	page 22
Watching Rain	page 42
I Am Alone	page 46
Birds Fly	page 50
Jade, You Have Been Here	page 58
These Young Boys	page 62
Imagination	page 68
The Morning	page 74
Understand	page 78
I Truly Love Starry Nights	page 82
By The Sea	page 86
Smooth And Easy	page 90
My Friend Has A Hard Time	page 94
I Can Hear You	page 96
Withered Leaves	page 100
Screams	page 106

This Book is Dedicated

To

Carrie L. Brewer

You dazzle me with all you have accomplished
Thank you for your loyalty, dedication, and time
I believe in your magic
As we ride the roller coaster together.

Contents

Chapter Snapshots From One's Heart .... page 1
    I Traveled The World .... page 2
    Here .... page 2
    Scars .... page 3
    The Warmth I Feel .... page 3
    When I am Hurting .... page 4
    Hard To Fathom .... page 4
    For Years And Years .... page 5
    What Matters How Bright The Moon .... page 6
    I Am Young .... page 6
    The Two Of Us .... page 7
    I Love .... page 7
    My Dad .... page 8
    Your Smell Lingers .... page 8
    We Kissed .... page 9
    Slow Genle Kiss .... page 11
    Spectacular .... page 11
    Reciprocal Love .... page 12
    Once You Are Hurt .... page 12
    A Solar Flare .... page 13

Chapter Gentle Fondness Comes With A Quiet Touch .... page 15
    Little Did He Know .... page 16
    Today .... page 16
    I Came In .... page 17
    Find Me .... page 19
    The Gift .... page 19
    We Made It .... page 19
    Once .... page 20
    Over Time .... page 20
    Cats Have .... page 21

Chapter Laughter In Brief Moments .... page 23
    Joys In Life .... page 24
    Best Thing About .... page 24

Dieting	page 25
I have A Need For A Hammer	page 25
Truth Comes Easy	page 26
Husband	page 26
My Hotel Room	page 27
Today	page 27
Scale	page 28
Angry	page 28
What I Want	page 29
The Laugh	page 29
Realize	page 30
Determined To Start My Diet	page 30
I Am So Lonely	page 31
Always Trying To Lose Weight	page 31
I Need An Angel	page 31
Love Takes Time	page 32
My Perfect Combination	page 32
If You Ever Leave Me	page 32
I Called	page 33
Boyfriends	page 33
Going Into The Marriage	page 34
How Fast Can You Leave	page 35
Somewhere	page 35
By The Way	page 36
Once In A While	page 36
Gossip Is Unverifiable	page 37
I Want To Live Long Enough	page 37

Chapter Lifetime Happenings ....page 38

God Whispered In My Ear	page 39
Relationship	page 39
To Know	page 40
She Is Dead	page 40
Watching Rain	page 41
Suspenseful Life	page 43
Misery Comes	page 43
Addiction	page 44
It's Your Own Damn Fault	page 44

I Am Alone	page 45
I Hope	page 47
The Fight Begins	page 48
Birds Fly	page 49
I Had Enough Of Your Bull Shit	page 51
Yesterday	page 51
We Broke Up	page 52
Being Apart Hurts	page 52
Soul Housed	page 53
In The End	page 53
My Sisters And I	page 54

Chapter Kids Giggling As They Play With Thoughts .... page 55

Bringing Up A Child	page 56
Excitement For Two	page 56
Jade, You Have Been Here	page 57
My Teenager Screwed Up	page 59
So Small Am I	page 59
To Dad	page 60
Jade Loves My Nativity Scene	page 60
These Young Boys	page 61

Chapter Essence Of Life In Abbreviation .... page 63

Watch How A Loser Behaves	page 64
Writing	page 64
Defending Traditions	page 65
Treat Yourself	page 65
New Year Resolutions	page 66
Baggage We Carry And Carry	page 66
Imagination	page 67
Two Ways	page 69
Problems	page 69
My Tears	page 70
He Is Losing His Hearing	page 70
My Thoughts	page 71
I Do Not Want To Say Hello	page 71
Look We All Make Mistakes	page 72
I Am Working	page 72
This Morning	page 73

Beware of Indifference	page 75
Hopefully	page 75
I Am A Simple	page 76
It Is A Gift	page 76
Understand	page 77
This Is Your Time	page 79
I Am	page 79
I Write	page 79
Fight For	page 80
Humbled	page 80
If I Dwell	page 80
I Truly Love Starry Nights	page 81
Do You Know What You Want	page 83
I Recorded My	page 83

Chapter Nature's Happenings .... page 84

By The Sea	page 85
Gentle Rain	page 87
It is Twilight	page 87
This Year I Will	page 88
Saturday	page 88
Smooth And Easy	page 89
Five Forty-Six	page 91
Gentle Rain	page 91
What's With The Heat	page 92
My Friend Has A Hard Time	page 93
I Can Hear You	page 95
Making Love With The Bugs	page 97
So Many Ways To	page 98
Winter	page 98
Withered Leaves	page 99

Chapter Finishing Is A Win .... page 101

No	page 102
Biggest Fight	page 103
We Have Different Talents	page 104
Screams	page 105

There Always

Is a door

Open

Emerge

Life awaits

Snapshots From One's Heart

I Traveled The World

In the most intimate way

Never leaving home

Warm and comfortable

In bed

For it is all in books.

Here

Do you care

I am alone

Struggling, for you

To be here.

Scars

Souvenirs that last

Longer than the wound

The Warmth I Feel

When I know I am loved

And needed

When I Am Hurting

I want my mother to comfort me

When hurt is brought on

By my mother

I cry alone.

Hard To Fathom

When I care

For there is

No assurance

She cares.

For Years And Years

I have loved you

With full knowledge

Of love, that is not returned.

Only I can tell the tale

Of the heart in turmoil,

Dark loneliness

In the light of day

Of one's love

That only kisses in the night.

What Matters How Bright The Moon

What matters, the power of the howling wind

What matters, how brightly shines the sun

When love is in focus

Nothing else matters.

I Am Young

A young poet at that

I can disappear in a crowd, and

On my own

Allowing

A shadow

To always

Remain.

The Two Of Us

Bound for life

Chance meeting

From across the room.

I Love

She does not,

Those sweet kisses

Will never be.

My Dad

Had sunshine

Hanging around

As if sunshine

Enjoyed lingering

With him

Your Smell Lingers

Long after you left

Would forget you faster

If you took your smell with you

We Kissed

No one will see

For this kiss

Belongs to the night

With all its stars,

Bright moon,

Gentle breeze, and

Our hearts.

Slow Gentle Kiss

Easy, smooth, and enticing

Upon my waiting lips

Wanting forever

Settle for the night

Spectacular

The gentle touch of a lover

Reciprocal Love

We gave up

Part of ourselves

To have

Reciprocal love

Once You Are Hurt

By love

You learn love's importance

A Solar Flare

Electrifying through every inch of me

The force, astonishing

Enjoyed

Now a vapor, fragile and fleeting.

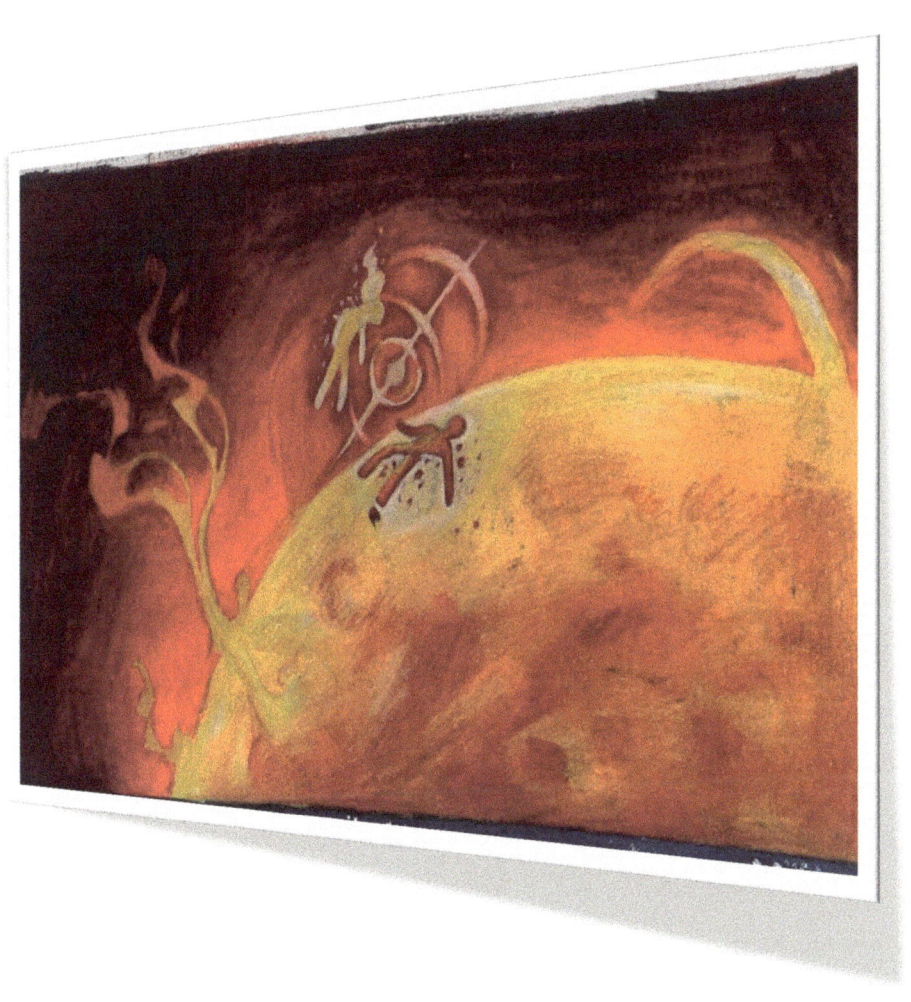

Gentle Fondness Comes
With A
Quiet Touch

Little Did He Know

Who I was

Nor did I know, who he was.

That is why, we should not hurry love

Little did we know.

Today

When I thought all sensuousness

Was gone for good

It came today

Along with the sunrise

And warm dreams.

The mood so very perfect

No need to rise

We stay put under the covers

Before winter arrives.

I Came In

From the rain

When I did not

Want to.

Find Me

I want to be touched

The Gift

Of love

It's better than

A brand-new car

A diamond ring

For love, is the

Reason for

The gift.

We Made It

One more day

Together

Once

My skin so soft

Gentle to the touch

Wanting to be felt.

Now, the same skin

Has wrinkles

With ridges, able to be seen

In every picture taken

Rough to the touch

Yet

Wanting touch more

Than ever.

Over Time

The marvel quiets to routine

Cats Have

Their own way of showing affection

If they even show affection

Cats give off a hint of contentment

The softest, almost inaudible

purr.

Laughter In Brief Moments

Joys In Life

I need them

Otherwise, I would never

Get out of bed.

This morning the

Smell of bacon cooking

Got me up.

Best Thing About

Eating spaghetti

Is the slurping

Dieting

Putting food

On

Your spouse's plate

I Have A Need For A Hammer

To destroy the demons that

Enter my dreams

Truth Comes Easy

After forty-seven

Can't remember lies

Husband

Would do anything for me

Except change

My Hotel Room

Always needs cleaning

It's the messy in me

That keeps the sign on the door

Do Not Disturb

Today

I think it is best

Not to think of ourselves

We know too much

Scale

Yes, I get on it every day

My way of dieting

If it's more, I do not eat

If it's less, I eat everything

Angry

Enough to put

Me on the couch

Not for a nap

To be analyzed

What I Want

I am in my declining years

Able to decline everything I do not like

Well, almost everything

Still get the annual flu shot.

The Laugh

That took us by surprise

At Stella's funeral

They played

The wicked witch is dead

Realize

At sixty-two

I do not look

As good

As when I was twenty-six.

So, I stopped

Looking in the mirror.

Determined To Start My Diet

As requested by Dr. Neff

Just

Not today.

I Am So Lonely

That when my computer

Writes in script

"hello"

I wait until

The entire word is written.

Always Trying To Lose Weight

I think it might be easier to grow taller!

I Need An Angel

To sit upon my right shoulder

To help me stop

Wasting my time with toxic people

Love Takes Time

Lust needs none

My Perfect Combination

Red wine, warm bread, and olive oil.

If You Ever Leave Me

I am going with you

I Called

To report

My lost credit card,

They ask

What's your number?

Hello, are you listening?

I lost my credit card.

Boyfriends

Like hot dogs

Never know what

They are made of, nor what

Effects this hot dog

Will have on you.

Going Into The Marriage

I felt like a brand-new car

After the wedding, I felt like

I lost 20% of my value.

As our third anniversary approached,

I know I am like an old, used car, I keep going,

Ever so often, I break down

(Yet most of the time, reliable).

How Fast Can You Leave

That is what I am thinking

When love is over

Somewhere

I will meet

My grandkids

As

They get taller

I get shorter

By The Way

When you read poems with rising heat

You are

Really thinking about sex.

Once In A While

I look in the mirror

Stunned by the reflection

Where has time gone?

Gossip Is Unverifiable

So what?

It's lots of fun

I Want To Live Long Enough

So that my last check bounces.

So said my brother, Chris.

Lifetime Happenings

God Whispered In My Ear

He promised, good coming my way

Was it the whisper

My hard work

For

Good came my way.

Relationship

Embraced with desire

And

The fantasy of forever

To Know

There is hardly any time

Left of me

She Is Dead

Her scarf filled with her smell

To hold me together

A bit longer

Watching Rain

Falls upon my heart

Thunder comes, that

Wakes my sorrows

Suspenseful Life

Not knowing

What will be

Tomorrow

Misery Comes

To all

Even happy people

Addiction

Buries your dreams

Disconnects with all

Your relationships.

Lastly, forgetting

Who you are.

It's Your Own Damn Fault

You knew right from wrong

You choose wrong repeatedly

I Am Alone

Among so many

I Hope

People will remember me

Not for what I did wrong.

Remember the day

I held your hand

I helped

I cared

I wept

For your loss.

The Fight Begins

Over things

Her Will read;

Divide everything between

The four of you

Listing her kids' names.

We did argue

Not that we wanted everything

The only thing left of mom

Were her things

We had to share the last of

Mom.

Birds Fly

Fish swim

Goats climb

Music stops

While I grieve

I Had Enough Of Your Bull Shit

Why I didn't tell my spouse that, the first year of marriage.

Fifteen years into the marriage, I finally figured it out

There was nothing to fear

I was not a kid, nor he my parent.

Yesterday

Is over

I can learn from yesterday

Not live by yesterday

We Broke Up

For the most part

We neutralized

Our everything

Being Apart Hurts

For I miss

How we were as

Us

Soul Housed

In a very secure space

Purely for protection

So well secured, not even

I know its location.

In The End

As well as the beginning

It is really you alone

On the stage of life

My Sisters And I

Having a talk

We want to know

If we must behave

During the months of

June, July, and September

Months before Christmas.

Yes, we want to know

In the middle of the year

Do we have to behave

For gifts from Santa.

Kids Giggling As They Play With Thoughts

Bringing Up A Child

There are a lot of things

That must go right

To come out right.

I want the formula

Right now, things are not going

The right way.

Excitement For Two

The first time you see your son's

Face, filled with excitement,

For he figured out those

Colorful wooden blocks

Can build

A tall building!

Jade, You Have Been Here

For three weeks

You have yet to do

The dishes

Take out the garbage

Hang the towels up

You are late every day.

I assure you, this invitation was

The last.

My Teenager Screwed Up

He now wants

The telling to be the only

Consequence.

So Small Am I

Hardly noticed by the world

Yet Puppy-Dog knows

Me, well enough for all.

To Dad

Who never cared

About his kids being

Girls or boys.

We were always

Treated the same

Jade Loves My Nativity Scene

For the last four or five years he arranges

All the main participants

This year, he brought my nativity scene

A gift

His yellow plastic toy hippo.

These Young Boys

I watch as they play ball

I know there is not a single thought

Of growing old and gray

Essence of Life
In Abbreviation

Watch How A Loser Behaves

Watch how a person with power behaves

It is the test of character

Writing

Says a lot about who I am

Words I do not write

Says a lot about

Me too

Defending Traditions

From one generation to the next

Impacts my mortality

Treat Yourself

Now that you're mid-way

Through life

Give your impulses

A good time

New Year Resolutions

Keep in mind

Be gentle with yourself

The benefits of resolutions

Are the doing, not the listing

Baggage We Carry And Carry

Risking moving forward

From the weight of our baggage

From the encroaching past

Imagination

Scary

Imagination craves excitement

Two Ways

To face our world

One, with courage

One, with fear

Choose wisely.

Problems

Fixable

If you admit to having

Them.

My Tears

Kept in a glass jar

For safe keeping

Wanting to remember

I cried

He Is Losing His Hearing

Or is it that I mumble too softly

Either way, we are

Unable to hear each other

Only our touch is noticed.

My Thoughts

Very active

Reason for sleepless nights

So robust, and active

I need the trick, to turn

Thinking off.

I Do Not Want To Say Hello

Especially to a new year

Hate to recognize the

Passage of time.

Look We All Make Mistakes

So what?

That is part of being human

Figure out forgiveness

Not lose tomorrow too.

I Am Working

Always to tell the truth

Takes a bit of time

To have the lies fade.

This Morning

The sun was beaming in my window

Its purpose, to wake me up

On a happy note.

Beware of Indifference

For

Indifference has no fertilizer

For blooming

Hopefully

Tomorrow will be better

No matter what is going wrong

I Am A Simple

Woman

That loves

Walking in the mornings

Reading in the afternoons

Intwined with my love in the evenings.

Parting in the works

For your evenings were not with me.

It is A Gift

Not a demand

Understand

That there is no perfect

Relationship

The ups, need to be higher

Than the downs, are lower.

This Is Your Time

Acknowledge

There is a limit to your time

Engage in every moment.

I Am

Remember

You are too.

I Write

To hide

All that

Troubles me.

The times I am happy

I cannot spare

The time to write.

Fight For

Acceptance of our differences

Dignity to follow

Humbled

By my heroes

Because they helped

Me

When in need

Without thought of

Repayment

If I Dwell

On sadness

I will

Lose happy moments

I Truly Love Starry Nights

I get to think of who I may know

Staring down at me.

The thought that as each of us leave

We are given a star

To shine for eons.

My guess, it is mom

Doing her best to outshine

Every star, just so we can visit.

Do You Know What You Want

Or need?

Beware

Others will or can

Make the choice for you.

Take care

Know what you want

Know

What you need.

I Recorded My

Dad and Uncle Nick

Singing

Vagabond Lover

What a warm

Treasure to play and

To replay.

Nature's Happenings

By The Sea

I hear the voice

Of the sea;

Be still

Listen.

The sea's voice

Quiets, one's soul.

Gentle Rain

Falling

Upon my face

As if the rain is

Right from heaven

It is Twilight

Walk with me, my lady

The world is awaiting

Us

To put our love into verse.

This Year I Will

Water my garden

Hidden within me

Saturday

Morning, I am at the beach

Watching the sunrise

A little intimacy

Noticed.

Smooth And Easy

The walk into the woods

With my favorite people

Me, myself, and I

Mother nature, my guide.

Five Forty-Six

Saturday morning

I am at the beach

Watching the sunrise

Gentle Rain

Softly falling, down

Upon my face

God, please

No changes wanted.

What's With The Heat

It is sweltering

It is my summer nightmare

A fan does not cool me off

Nor, the morning swim.

To cool down, I need

The air conditioner

At sixty-nine degrees

Nothing else works.

Cool times, a must

Hate to see the

Coming electric bill.

My Friend Has A Hard Time

Making a decision

I tend to think

If she had a tree

Full of red apples,

All the apples the same

She would still question

"Which one do I pick?"

I Can Hear You

Over the roar of

Incoming waves

As I walk the beach

We once walked

Hand in hand.

Making Love With The Bugs

We were hot for each other

Nothing was going to stop us

We kissed, and we kissed

As the bugs bit. and bit.

We came away, with hundreds of bites

Between the two of us

Knowing full well, we had

Something more than bug bites.

So Many Ways To

Wander into the woods

To find the secrets nature

Has in store for you.

Do listen without fear

Play the game with nature

The winners can close their eyes

Realizing nature can always be

A part of you.

Winter

The time of year

To cuddle and huddle

In the night's quiet time

Listening for the snow to fall

Withered Leaves

Dark with rot

Drench in moist murkiness

Decay has started

To do its magic

To Bring life

To waiting seeds

Finishing Is A Win

No

Torture

You get

From me

Is Enough.

For the hurt

For the wounds

For the indignity

For the lost dreams

You gave me so freely,

Every torture I can think of

Is worthless, meaningless and

Takes up too much of my limited time

Of which, I have already lost so much of.

You little bastard

Biggest Fight

I want it over

Or part with great pains

For marriage is not a race, a game

Nor a contest.

We must figure out

How to make it work

Or part with great pains.

For this in not a race

A game, nor a contest

But our life,

To keep in touch with each other's heart

Or part with great pains.

We Have Different Talents

Born in different countries with

Different ancestors

Yet somehow, we are together

Our lives have touched

As we journey

On the same road.

Screams

Heard from afar

Yet

They were mine

Silent to the world

Casting shadows

Complicating my life

And disturbing my sleep.